THE WATERS OF LIFE

— ✦ The facts and the fables ✦ —

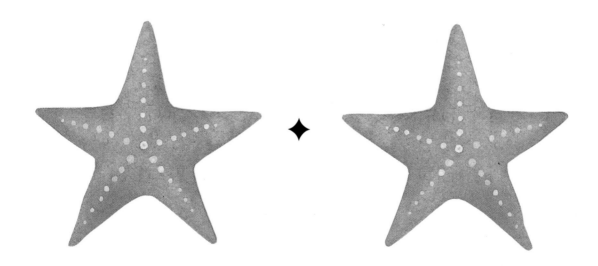

Finn Bevan
Illustrated by Diana Mayo

CHILDREN'S PRESS ®
A Division of Grolier Publishing
NEW YORK • LONDON • HONG KONG • SYDNEY
DANBURY, CONNECTICUT

Text © Finn Bevan 1997
Illustrations © Diana Mayo 1997

First American Edition by
Children's Press
A Division of Grolier Publishing Co., Inc.
Sherman Turnpike
Danbury, Connecticut 06813

Series editor: Rachel Cooke
Art director: Robert Walster
Designer: Mo Choy
Picture research: Sue Mennell

A CIP catalog record for this book is available from the Library of Congress.

Printed in Singapore

Picture acknowledgements:
Ancient Art & Architecture Collection pp. 7, 27 (Johan Adlercreutz);
Werner Forman Archive p. 11 (private collection);
Robert Harding pp. 14, 16
Hutchison Library p. 22

Contents

Water, Water Everywhere

Water plays an essential part in all our lives. It is the giver of life itself—without it, the world simply could not survive. Seas, lakes, and rivers provide people with water for drinking and crops and a plentiful source of food. Many myths and legends have grown up around these waters, as people seek to explain their great significance and to explore the way they shape our lives.

Waters of Life

Rivers and seas are to be both feared and respected by the people who live along their shores. All of a sudden, the sea can change, from glassy calm to crashing waves. Before they understood the scientific reasons for these changes, people saw them as the actions of the gods and spirits who inhabited the waters of life.

The gods and spirits controlled the waves, tides, and floods. It was vital to keep them happy and contented. Ancient sailors never set sail without first praying to the gods of the sea to grant them safe passage.

Many great civilizations, such as that of ancient Egypt, grew up along rivers. The river gods were all important. If they were angry and sent no water for the fields, the harvest would fail and people would starve.

In many cultures and religions, water is believed to have holy powers to heal people and wash away their sins. People often wash before they enter a holy place, or touch their foreheads with water. In Christianity, people are baptized with water to mark the start of their new, religious lives. Jesus Christ himself was baptized in the waters of the Jordan River in Israel.

The Sacred River

From its source in an ice cave high in the Himalayas, the Ganges River flows south-east across India for 1,540 miles (2,480 km) until it reaches the Bay of Bengal and the sea. For Hindus, this is their most sacred river, worshipped as the goddess, Ganga. They believe that bathing in the Ganges River cleanses their souls and washes away their sins. This brings them closer to salvation. Millions of pilgrims flock to the river to bathe.

The Holiest City

Many big cities have grown up along the banks of the Ganges. One of these is Varanasi. This is the holiest city for Hindus, where the water of the Ganges is particularly sacred and powerful. Devout Hindus try to visit Varanasi at least once in their lives to bathe in the river. People also come to Varanasi to die, as dying there is believed to bring instant salvation.

*An 10th-century
bronze statue
of Shiva dancing*

City of Shiva

Legend says that Lord Shiva chose
Varanasi to stand at the very center
of Earth. It was his favorite home
on Earth where he lived with his
wife Parvati. All over the city
there are temples and shrines
dedicated to Lord Shiva.

Steps of Salvation

Steep, crumbling steps, called *ghats*,
lead down to the river. These are
crowded with pilgrims and priests.
There are temples and shrines at
every step. One of the most important
ghats is called Manikarna Ghat. At the
top of the steps is a tank full of water.
Legend says that Parvati dropped
her earring here and Shiva dug
the tank to get it back, filling it
with his sweat as he worked.

How the Ganges Fell to Earth

This is the story of how the sacred Ganges, the river of heaven, came down from heaven to Earth.

There was once a king called Bhagiratha. He was a very holy man and spent many years in the holy Himalayan mountains, praying to the great god, Shiva.

King Bhagiratha had a special horse, a mighty beast with a glossy black coat and a jet-black mane, given to him by the gods. It was his greatest pride and joy. One day, the demons came and stole the horse and, to King Bhagiratha's great dismay, carried it off to the dark depths of the underworld.

Now King Bhagiratha had 60,000 sons and nephews. "We will find the horse and bring it back," they said. But as they dug deeper and deeper into the Earth, they were burned to ashes by the terrible heat.

The King called on Lord Shiva. "Please, Lord," he begged, "let the sacred river fall from the sky and bring my sons and nephews back to life."

Shiva agreed. He ordered the river to fall to Earth from its heavenly source in Lord Vishnu's toe. But as the mighty waters began to crash downwards, King Bhagiratha had a terrible thought. If the water hit the ground, the Earth would surely shatter under its weight? What could be done to prevent this disaster?

Once again, Lord Shiva came to the rescue. As the Ganges fell to Earth, he caught the rushing river in the tangled locks of his long, thick hair, then let it trickle in a gentle stream down to the Himalayas. Then King Bhagiratha carefully led the Ganges from the mountains, over the plains, across the sea, and deep down in the underworld, to the kingdom of the dead. Here its sacred waters touched the ashes of his sons and nephews and brought them back to life. The jet-black horse was never seen again. But King Bhagiratha was so happy to have his sons and nephews back, he didn't really mind too much. And to this day the Ganges flows from the Himalayas to the sea, bringing life-giving water to India.

Taming the Tides

MONGOLIA

JAPAN

KOREA

CHINA

PACIFIC
OCEAN

EAST
CHINA SEA

Twice a day, every day, the sea rises and flows on to the shore. Twice a day, the water ebbs, or falls, away again. These daily changes in sea level are called the tides. Today we know that the tides are caused by a force called gravity. But for many ancient peoples, including those of China and Japan, they were controlled by the gods.

How Tides Happen

Tides are caused by the pull of the Moon's gravity on the Earth. This makes the water in the oceans wash back and forth across the Earth, like water slopping back and forth in a gigantic bowl. At high tide, the water rises and laps on to the shore. At low tide, it ebbs away again. Tides are also affected by the Earth's spin.

Dragon Kings

In Chinese mythology, the four seas which lie
around the Earth are each ruled by a Dragon
King. The four Dragon Kings live in crystal
palaces, deep under the waves and
filled with precious treasures.
From here, they control
the tides, waves, and
everything in the sea
and on the shore.

The Old Man of the Tide

In Japanese mythology, there are
many gods of the sea. The greatest is
O-Wata-Tsu-Mi, the Old Man of the Tide. He
controls the tides and waves. His servants include
the god of the seabed, the god of the middle waters
and the god of the surface. These gods rule over all the
fish and other creatures in the sea, and have the power to
speed sailors on their way or send storms to wreck their
ships. Their messenger is a fearsome sea monster, Wani.

The Gift of the Tides

This is a Japanese story of how the tides came to be.

◆

There were once two princes, Fireshine and Fireshade, the great grandsons of the goddess of the Sun. Prince Fireshine was a fisherman; his brother a hunter. One day, Prince Fireshade had a bright idea.

"I know," he told his brother. "Let's swap places. I'm fed up with hunting."

So the two brothers changed places and Fireshade borrowed his brother's best fish-hook and set off for the sea. But fishing was hard—not only did Fireshade catch no fish but he also lost his brother's fish-hook. It sank down and down, to the depths of the sea. His brother Fireshine was furious.

"Just go and fetch it back," he ordered.

So Prince Fireshade dived to the bottom of the sea and reached the palace of the Old Man of the Tide. He had a warm welcome—the sea god helped him find the lost fish-hook and also gave him the hand of his daughter in marriage.

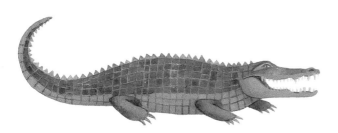

The time came for Prince Fireshade to return to the land with his bride. With great sadness and sorrow, the sea god bid them farewell. As a parting gift, he gave Fireshade two magic jewels, one to make the sea waters rise and the other to make them fall again. Then Fireshade and his wife left the sea, riding on a crocodile.

When Fireshade gave the fish-hook back to his brother, he thought he would be pleased. But Fireshine still blamed him for being so careless. To spite his brother, Fireshade took out the tide jewels. He threw one jewel into the sea. The waters rose up and crashed on to shore. Terrified, Fireshine begged his brother to stop; he would never mention the fish-hook again. So Fireshade threw the other jewel into the sea. The water ebbed away and calm returned. And the brothers agreed to be friends again.

Then Prince Fireshade collected the jewels from the sea, in case he needed to use them again. And this is how the tides came to be.

Legends of the Lake

In the Andes Mountains lies Lake Titicaca, the highest large lake in the world. On the border of Peru and Bolivia, the lake is 12,507 ft (3,812 m) above sea level. It is 112 miles (180 km) long, 45 miles (72 km) wide and covers an area of over 3,000 square miles (8,000 km^2). For the Incas who once ruled the region, the lake was a sacred place. It was here, they believed, that their ancestors first came to Earth.

Reed Islands

Lake Titicaca is dotted with islands of reeds, called *totora*. On some of the islands are the ancient ruins of Inca settlements; on others, present-day villages. The reeds are used to make baskets and boats used for fishing and transportation.

Inca Beliefs

The dramatic landscape of the Andes often featured in the Incas' myths and legends. Sacred places were known as *huacas*. Lake Titicaca was one of their greatest *huacas*—the place of the ancestors and, according to one legend, the home of Viracocha, the Incas' creator god.

Island in the Lake

This myth tells how the ancestors of all the Incas
came to Earth in the middle of Lake Titicaca.

◆

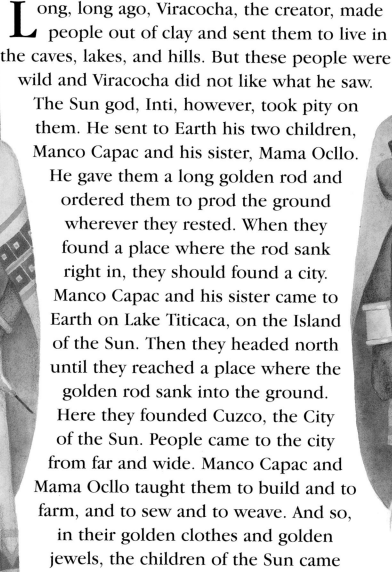

Long, long ago, Viracocha, the creator, made people out of clay and sent them to live in the caves, lakes, and hills. But these people were wild and Viracocha did not like what he saw. The Sun god, Inti, however, took pity on them. He sent to Earth his two children, Manco Capac and his sister, Mama Ocllo. He gave them a long golden rod and ordered them to prod the ground wherever they rested. When they found a place where the rod sank right in, they should found a city. Manco Capac and his sister came to Earth on Lake Titicaca, on the Island of the Sun. Then they headed north until they reached a place where the golden rod sank into the ground. Here they founded Cuzco, the City of the Sun. People came to the city from far and wide. Manco Capac and Mama Ocllo taught them to build and to farm, and to sew and to weave. And so, in their golden clothes and golden jewels, the children of the Sun came from Lake Titicaca to be the first rulers of the Incas.

Fighting the Floods

Many people live along the banks of great rivers. They rely on them to water their fields, but they also greatly fear floods. When the water rises out of control, crops can be devastated, people left homeless and lives lost. Early Chinese civilization grew up around two great rivers —the Yangtze (or Chang Jiang) and the Yellow (or Huang He). There are many Chinese myths that show the awesome power of floods.

Tales of Two Rivers

The Yangtze is China's longest river and the third longest in the world. It stretches for 3,900 miles (6,300 km) from the Tanggula Mountains in the west to the East China Sea. It is vitally important for transporting goods and people, and for watering the rice paddy fields. Millions of people live along its banks.

The Yellow River gets its name from the yellow silt that colors its waters.

Every few years, the Yangtze and Yellow Rivers burst their banks, with disastrous results. In 1887, the Yellow River flooded, with the loss of up to seven million lives. This is the greatest flood ever known.

The Great Flood

In Chinese mythology, anyone with the power to control a flood was held in great respect. One story tells of a flood sent by the gods to destroy the world. One of the gods, Gun, saw how much people were suffering and took pity on them. He managed to stop the flood by throwing a lump of magic soil into the water where it grew into mountains and dry land.

The other gods were furious. They killed Gun and sent another flood, even greater than the last. But Gun has a son, called Yu, who carried on his father's task. He turned himself into a yellow dragon and drained all the water back into the sea. As a reward for his courage, Yu was made the first emperor of China.

The Gourd Children and the Flood

This Chinese story tells of the Thunder God and a mighty flood.

One hot summer's day, a long time ago, a farmer was busy working in his fields. Suddenly, the sky grew dark and he heard a loud rumble of thunder.

"Quick! Get indoors," he told his children, a girl and boy. "The storm will soon be here."

And in they ran. The farmer hung a big iron cage on a hook by the door, and followed them inside. Sure enough, the storm soon began. Thunder boomed, lightning flashed and rain fell in torrents. The farmer took down a sharp spear from the wall, which he used to catch tigers, opened the door of the big iron cage and waited . . .

With a mighty crash, the Thunder God flew down from the clouds, his fearsome battle-axe in his hand. Quick as could be, the farmer stabbed the god with his tiger spear, pushed him into the cage and shut the door with a bang. As soon as he did this, the rain stopped, the storm died down and the Sun began to shine.

The farmer had plans for the Thunder God, to stop his mischief once and for all. He'd kill him, then he'd pickle him. He went to market to buy some sauce and spices. As he left home, he said to his children: "Whatever you do, don't give the Thunder God any water to drink. No matter how thirsty he says he is."

As soon as the farmer set off down the path, the Thunder God seized his chance. "Children, good children, nice children," he whined. "Could you possibly spare a drop of water? I'm so thirsty, so thirsty."

At first, the children refused. They remembered what their father had said. But the Thunder God went on and on, for longer than either of them could bear so finally they granted him his wish. But no sooner had he drunk a sip, than the Thunder God revived and broke out of his cage.

"You've both been very helpful," he told the children, with a sly grin. "And this is your reward . . ." And he pulled a tooth right out of his mouth and told them to plant it in the ground. Then he flew away.

The children dug a small hole and planted the tooth, as the Thunder God had said. And immediately, before their eyes, a plant began to grow and on it was a large, round, hollow gourd. Then the sky grew dark and the thunder rumbled overhead. The rain poured and the flood waters began to rise.

This was the sight that
greeted the farmer when he got back
from market. He told the children to get into the
gourd, while he himself got into his little wooden boat.
Then they sailed up to heaven to beg the Lord of Heaven for
help. The Lord of Heaven granted their wishes. He summoned the
Water God and ordered him to end the flood. "Yes, Your Majesty,"
grovelled the Water God. "At once, Your Majesty."
In his hurry to obey the Lord of Heaven, the Water God made the
floodwaters fall away so suddenly that the farmer's boat crashed to Earth and
he was killed. But the children floated safely down in their gourd. They were
the only people to survive the terrible flood. But they lived happily and became
the ancestors of everyone else that lived on Earth.

The Gift of the Nile

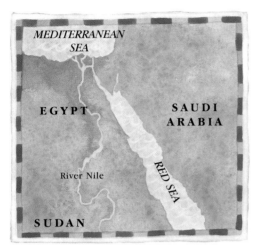

Floods were not always to be feared. For the ancient Egyptians, their very lives depended on them. The Nile River was their major source of water, for farming and drinking. All around it lay desert, parched, sandy, and dry. Most important of all was the river's annual flood. As the waters rose, they covered the fields with rich, black mud, the ideal soil in which crops could grow.

The Nile River

The Nile is the longest river in the world. It flows for 4,143 miles (6,671 km) from its source near the Equator, across north-east Africa, until it reaches the Mediterranean Sea where it forms a huge, spreading delta. All along its course, the Nile irrigates (waters) large strips of farmland. But the building of the Aswan High Dam in Egypt means it no longer floods as it did in ancient times.

The Farmers' Year

In ancient Egypt, the farming year was based around the annual floods.

1. The river flooded from July to November. Farming stopped and the farmers worked for the Pharaoh, building or mining.

2. From December to March, the waters fell back and the farmers ploughed and sowed their fields.

4. Then it was time to repair the irrigation canals ready for the next flood.

3. The crops were harvested in March and April.

God of the Nile

The ancient Egyptians did not know that the real reason for the annual flood was melting snow and rain high up in the mountains of Ethiopia. This sent great torrents of water rushing down the river. They believed that the flood was caused by the god, Hapi. Hapi was one of hundreds of gods worshipped by the ancient Egyptians. Some ruled over nature, others over daily life. Carvings and paintings of Hapi show him wearing a fisherman's belt and a headdress of water plants. In his hands he often carries a tray of food, riches provided by the life-giving Nile.

How Hapi Was Set Free

This is the story of how Hapi was released from his prison so that the Nile could rise again.

Long, long ago, in the reign of King Zoser, disaster struck. For seven long years, the Nile River did not rise. The floodwaters failed and the fields were left parched, brown, and dry. With no harvest to gather, and little to eat, the people of Egypt were close to starving.

"We beseech you, Pharaoh," they begged the King. "Find the water and bring it back. Otherwise we shall all surely die."

The King thought long and hard. He summoned his chief priest, Imhotep. If anyone could solve the problem, it was he.

"We must do something," he told the priest. "And quickly."

Imhotep set off along the river, to an island called Elephantine, where he knew the god Hapi had his home. For he was the god who controlled the flood and made the river rise. Perhaps he was angry and so had stopped the water rising? With him, Imhotep had all sorts of offerings to please the god and persuade him to change his mind.

But a surprise lay in store for noble Imhotep. As he approached the caves where Hapi lived, he found the doors locked and firmly bolted. And inside was Hapi. After a quarrel with Khnum, the ram god, he had been locked away as punishment. He'd been kept a prisoner for seven long years and only Khnum had the key. This was the reason why the floods had failed.

Imhotep knew what he had to do. He took his offerings, intended for Hapi, and presented them to Khnum instead, with all the prayers and praises he knew. That night, the ram-headed god appeared to King Zoser in a dream.

"Your priest has pleased me," he told the King. "I will set Hapi free. Do not fear any longer."

He was true to his word. The flood returned, the waters rose and the next year's harvest was the best ever seen.

Ruler of the Waves

EUROPE

GREECE

MEDITERRANEAN SEA

AFRICA

Ancient Greek civilization grew up around the shores of the Mediterranean. The sea was vital for trade and travel. The Greeks believed that the ocean flowed in a circle around the land, like a gigantic river. For many Greeks, the only part of the ocean that really mattered was the Mediterranean Sea. This marked the limits of the civilized world.

Prayers for Sailors

The ancient Greeks believed that everything in life and nature was controlled by the gods. The seas and oceans were no exception. They were ruled by mighty Poseidon, brother of Zeus, the Lord of the Gods. It was Poseidon who caused the storms and waves. Seafaring was a risky business. Before any voyage, long or short, a sailor first offered a sacrifice to Poseidon and prayed for safe sailing and calm seas.

Poseidon's Kingdom

Poseidon sped across the sea in a golden chariot, pulled by two tritons, who were half-man and half-fish. He lived in a fabulous golden palace deep beneath the waves. Shaggy haired and with a long beard, Poseidon was famous for his fiery temper. In his hand he carried a trident to summon or calm storms at sea. He was also the god of earthquakes.

The Temple of Poseidon high on the cliffs above Sunion Bay in Greece

Sea Nymphs

Nereus was a kindly old sea god, with seaweed for hair and the power to change into any shape he wished. He had 50 beautiful daughters, called the Nereids, or sea nymphs. They had the power to see into the future.'If a sailor caught a Nereid as she rode on her dolphin across the sea, he could force her to tell him the future in return for letting her go again. The most famous Nereid was Amphitrite, wife of Poseidon.

27

Poseidon, Athena, and Amphitrite

This is the story of how Poseidon quarrelled with Athena and won Amphitrite as his wife.

Life did not always run smoothly for Poseidon, God of the Sea. Although equal in all things to his brother, Zeus, it was Zeus who became Lord of the Gods and Ruler of Heaven, and not Poseidon. He was often heard to grumble that it simply wasn't fair.

His fiery temper got him into trouble with the other gods, too. Once he quarrelled with the goddess, Athena, over the naming of the greatest city in Greece. Neither would budge an inch. In the end, the people of the city suggested that each of the gods invent a gift. Whoever's gift was judged most useful would have the city named after them. So Poseidon struck a rock with his trident. A stream of seawater gushed from the rock and Poseidon promised the city great riches from sea trade if he won. As her gift to the city, Athena planted an olive tree. The olives could be eaten or used for oil. To Poseidon's fury, Athena was declared the winner and the city of Athens named in her honor. In a fit of spite, Poseidon flooded the city and the plains around it.

When it came to
finding a wife, however,
Poseidon had better luck. He fell in love
with the sea nymph, Amphitrite, when he saw her
one day dancing with her sisters. But when he asked
Amphitrite to marry him, she ran away. Poseidon sent one of his faithful
dolphins to find her. And when the dolphin brought her back, Poseidon was
so pleased he placed him in the sky as a star. From then on, Amphitrite was
always seen at her husband's side, riding in his golden chariot. They had two
daughters and a son, called Triton, who had the body of a human and a fish's
tail. He was said to cause the roar of the ocean by blowing through his conch
shell and gave his name to the two creatures who pulled Poseidon's chariot.

Notes and Explanations

Who's Who

ANCIENT EGYPTIANS: The people who lived in Egypt, along the banks of the Nile River, from about 5,000 to 30 BC. Famous for their temples, pyramids, and tombs, these have provided a huge amount of information about the myths, beliefs, and lifestyle of ancient Egypt. The ancient Egyptians worshipped many gods and goddesses who controlled all aspects of nature and daily life.

ANCIENT GREEKS: The people who lived in Greece from about 2,000 BC. Theirs was a highly advanced civilization, famous for its arts, science, and trade. Myths formed an important part of ancient Greek religion, explaining the nature of their gods. We know these myths through the works of ancient Greek writers such as the poet, Homer, who lived in about the 8th century BC.

CHRISTIANS: Followers of Jesus Christ, a teacher and preacher who lived 2,000 years ago in Palestine. He was sentenced to death for his beliefs and crucified on a cross. Christians believe Jesus is the son of God. Today there are about 200 million Christians worldwide. Their holy book is the Bible.

HINDUS: Followers of the Hindu religion, which began in India some 4,500 years ago. About 80 percent of Indians are Hindus. They believe in a wide variety of gods and in reincarnation (being born again after death). A Hindu's aim in life is to break free of the cycle of birth and rebirth, and gain salvation.

INCAS: The people who lived in the Andes mountains of South America. At the beginning of the 16th century, they ruled over an empire which covered much of modern-day Peru, Ecuador, Boliva, and Chile. By 1533, they themselves had been conquered by Spanish invaders. Their chief god was Viracocha, the creator.

YU: Yu was the first emperor of the Xia dynasty (royal family) of China who ruled from about 2205-2197BC. He was believed to have been born as a dragon.

What's What

Strictly speaking, fables, legends, and myths are all slightly different. But the three terms are often used to mean the same thing—a symbolic story or a story with a message.

FABLE: A short story, not based in fact, which often has animals as its central characters and a strong moral lesson to teach.

LEGEND: An ancient, traditional story based on supposed historical figures or events.

MYTH: A story which is not based in historical fact but which uses supernatural characters to explain natural phenomena, such as the weather, night and day, the rising tides, and so on. Before the scientific facts were known, ancient people used myths to make sense of the world around them.

DELTA: The area formed by some rivers as they reach the sea and drop their load of mud and sand. This forms islands which break the rivers up into many channels.

GRAVITY: An invisible force which pulls things towards each other. The larger the object the stonger its gravitional pull. Tides are caused by the pull of the Moon's gravity on the Earth.

IRRIGATION: The supply of water, usually by canal or pipe, to places beyond the reach of a natural water supply in order to grow crops.

PILGRIMS: People who make a special journey, or pilgrimage, to a sacred place as an act of religious faith and devotion. Sacred places include natural sites, such as rivers and mountains, and places connected with events in the history of a religion.

SALVATION: The state where a person is saved from sin, or breaks free of the cycle of birth and rebirth and becomes one with God.

Where's Where

The map below shows where in the world the places named in this book are found.

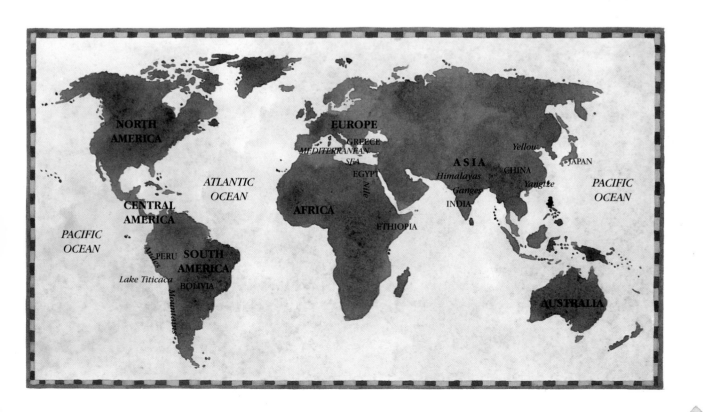

Index